家計簿 kakebo

This Book Belongs To: _____

Date: _____

First published by Giunti Editore S.p.A, Firenze-Milano, under the title
Kakebo. L'agenda dei conti di casa per risparmiare e gestire le tue spese senza stress

Kakebo. Copyright © 2016 by Giunti Editore S.p.A., Firenze-Milano, www.giunti.it

English text copyright © 2018 by HarperCollins Publishers

HarperCollins books may be purchased for educational, business, or sales promotional use. For information please email the Special Markets Department at SPsales@harpercollins.com.

Design and layout by Cinzia Chiari
Cover Design by Nancy Leonard

Published in 2018 by
Harper Design
An Imprint of HarperCollins*Publishers*
195 Broadway
New York, NY 10007
Tel: (212) 207-7000
Fax: (855) 746-6023
harperdesign@harpercollins.com
www.hc.com

Distributed throughout the world by
HarperCollins Publishers
195 Broadway
New York, NY 10007

ISBN 978-0-06-285796-5

Library of Congress Cataloging-in-Publication Data

Title: Kakebo: the Japanese art of mindful spending.
Description: New York: Harper Design, 2018.
Identifiers: LCCN 2018005411 | ISBN 9780062857965 (paperback)
Subjects: LCSH: Finance, Personal. | Happiness. | BISAC: BUSINESS & ECONOMICS
   / Personal Finance / Money Management. | BUSINESS & ECONOMICS / Budgeting.
Classification: LCC HG179 .K354 2018 | DDC 332.024—dc23
LC record available at https://lccn.loc.gov/2018005411

Printed in China

First Printing, 2018

家計簿

kakebo

The **JAPANESE ART**
of **MINDFUL SPENDING**

HARPER
DESIGN
An Imprint of HarperCollins Publishers

learn
about kakebo

The Japanese word *kakebo* (pronounced ka-kay-bo) literally means "household-accounts book." In Japan, everyone uses a kakebo—even little children are given their own specially designed books. At home and in school they learn to record their income and expenses.

Previous generations used to keep records of household income and expenses in their own notebooks. These days, with credit cards and payments made by cell phone—and one-click online shopping—we've lost track of the money moving in and out of our wallets. Kakebo is a useful and effective tool for keeping track of expenses and learning how to save.

5 good reasons
to use a kakebo

1) ORGANIZATION It's a useful tool for organizing your expenses by using a streamlined system that makes them easy to read.

2) CONTROL It helps you keep track of your daily expenses and rank them by how necessary they are.

3) SAVINGS It will help you save 20-30 percent more by helping you identify critical action items.

4) DISCIPLINE Writing down what you've spent by hand will lead you to stop buying things you don't need and help you develop willpower.

5) CONFIDENCE Keeping track of expenses makes you feel more secure and encourages you to trust your own skills. That reduces stress and helps you feel calm and relaxed.

break down expenses into categories

Kakebo lets you keep track of daily household spending by dividing expenses into four main categories: **Essential Expenses**, **Optional Expenses**, **Entertainment and Leisure**, and **Extras and Unforeseen Events**. Learn to break down your expenses in order to use your kakebo.

Essential Expenses

- **Supermarket:** food, body care, household cleaning supplies, etc.
- **Other food shopping:** food bought at farmers' markets, fish markets, produce markets, etc.
- **Pharmacy:** medicine, vitamins, and other specialized products.
- **Children:** baby food, diapers, school supplies, clothing, etc.
- **Transportation:** bus, train, and subway fares; parking fees; tolls, gas, etc.
- **Pets:** pet food, veterinary expenses, grooming, etc.
- **Cell phone expenses** (if you don't have a fixed monthly plan).

Optional Expenses

- **Shopping (adults):** new clothing, shoes, accessories, sporting goods, etc.
- **Cosmetics:** makeup, creams, nail polish, perfume, etc.
- **Taxis**
- **Gifts:** anniversary gifts, holiday gifts, birthday presents (this item can be significant if you have small children, who usually attend a lot of birthday parties).

Entertainment and Leisure

- **Books and magazines**
- **Music:** CDs, songs and videos.
- **Movies:** DVDs, theaters, streaming, etc.
- **Shows:** concerts, plays, festivals, etc.
- **Nightclubs and other entertainment**
- **Restaurants and takeout:** business lunches and lunches with family and friends, pizza, hamburgers, kebabs, and other snacks.
- **Cafés:** coffee and cocktails.
- **Pastry shops**

Extras and Unforeseen Events

- **Medical expenses:** doctor visits and tests, etc.
- **Childcare:** unless included under set costs.
- **Repairs:** electrician, plumber, mechanic, painter, etc.
- **Electronics:** computer, cell phone upgrade or replacement, television, camera, stereo system, etc.
- **Furnishings and housewares:** furniture, household appliances, cookware, linens, tools, etc.
- **Personal travel:** transportation, lodging, food, etc. If you travel frequently, you can include these expenses under Optional Expenses.

set a
monthly budget

At the start of the month, enter your income and fixed expenses. Calculate the difference between these two sums to find the total amount of money you'll have available during the month.

In this table note the date, item, and amount of **income** (salary and any other earnings) for the current month and add up the total. (See Advice for Special Situations on page 7.)

Write down all your **fixed expenses** here. Those are expenses that occur regularly: rent/mortgage payments, domestic help (cleaner, babysitter), gym membership, theater, cell phone (unless you use a pay-as-you-go plan), subscriptions and services like Netflix or Spotify, training, education, children's activities (sports, music lessons), parking fee, regular payments or installments, social security and other contributions, self-employment tax, etc.

Though you record your **UTILITIES** at the end of the month, you should be prepared to have a more limited budget during the period when the bills arrive.

month
April

record your monthly income and spending

income

date	item	amount
05	salary	$1,483
10	birthday gift	$247
30	storage space	$185
	rental income	
total income		**$1,915**

fixed expenses

rent/mortgage	$371		maintenance/HOA fees	$25
bus/subway pass	$31		parking space	$62
school/cafeteria			gym	$49
social insurance contributions			self-employment tax	
cell phone	$15			
childcare	$79			
total fixed expenses				**$632**

The **blank boxes** are to be used for any other fixed expenses, even if they're not monthly expenses (annual or quarterly). These may include car registration, maintenance or HOA fees, real estate taxes, etc.

Tip
It's a good idea to mark down **nonmonthly expenses** in the month when you pay the bill. If the amount is high, the best strategy is to divide the total and break it down over the months it covers. That way you'll be less stressed when it's time to pay the bill.

At the start of the month **set** short-term and long-term **goals** and draw up a list of ways to reach them (e.g., limit your use of taxis, buy coffee less frequently, and curb spending in the evenings).

goals and forecast

- Which expenses do you plan to cut to save money?

- How can you reach your goals?

How much do you want to save?   **$124**

How much money do you have available this month?

income	fixed expenses	forecast savings
$1,915	$632	$124

=

cash available   **$1,159**

You can also plan a **savings forecast** based on the amount you think you can save by implementing these new habits. Place the money in a piggy bank or, if you use online banking, transfer it to your savings account. The goal is to forget about it and not use it for your monthly expenses.

Advice for Special Situations

• If you are **self-employed**, you have two options for recording the invoices you've issued: you can base this number on all the invoices that were paid in the previous month, or you can base it on all the invoices that will come due in the current month. Choose either method; the important thing is to use the same method all year long.

• If your **salary** will be paid early in the following month, on the first day of that month, include an estimated amount based on the last salary (or stipend) you received.

• If you receive a **windfall**, you can keep part of this amount and record the income at the start of the following month (meaning it won't appear in the income for the current month). Or, if you don't need it this month, you can set the money aside in a piggy bank or in your savings account.

Subtract your fixed expenses from your income. If you plan to set some money aside, also subtract your forecast savings. This will help you determine how much cash you have available for the month. Consider this your **budget**.

add your
weekly expenses

Be consistent: Write down all your expenses in your kakebo every day. You should keep all the receipts from any purchases you make and write down your expenses each night before you go to bed. If you can't quite manage to do this daily, it is important to write in your kakebo at least twice a week and in the most extreme cases never less than once a week.

There is a column for each day.

The chart contains the four main expense categories:

Essential Expenses
This category includes your basic needs and other regular expenses.

Optional Expenses
This category includes expenses that are dispensable.

Entertainment and Leisure
This includes expenses for cultural activities, things you do in your free time, and entertainment.

Extras and Unforeseen Events
These are expenses that don't fall into a specific category, and can include emergencies and unexpected expenses such as repairs, furniture, computers, etc.

18 month **April**

	Monday 10	Tuesday 11	Wednesday	Thursday
essential expenses	supermarket $37		train $62	gas $25
optional expenses		lipstick $6		taxi $16 gift for Chiara $49
entertainment and leisure			pizza $9	lunch $19
extras and unforeseen events	cushion $25			
total	$62	$6	$71	$109

Record your **daily total** in the last row.

You'll use this amount to know how much cash you have available each week. The **change purse** for Week One will be the amount you have at the start of the month. The amount for Week Two will be the starting amount minus Week One's total expenses, and so on.

Number the weeks.

| week 1 | 🕐 $1,159 | 19 |

Friday	Saturday	Sunday	weekly expenses
oatmeal $6	ibuprofen $7		**essential expenses**
			supermarket $43
			other food
			pharmacy $7
			transportation $62
			children
			pets
			gas $25
			total $137
shoes $87	mascara $10		**optional expenses**
			shopping $87
			cosmetics $16
			gifts $49
			taxi $16
			total $168
breakfast in café $4 German book $31	dinner $37	movies $10	**entertainment and leisure**
			books & magazines $31
			music
			movies and shows $10
			cafés and takeout $13
			restaurants $56
			total $110
		weekend in Savannah $247	**extras and unforeseen events**
			medical expenses
			travel $247
			housewares $25
			total $272
$127	$54	$257	weekly total $686

You can use the **empty spaces** in the chart to include expenses that aren't listed. For example, if you use your car or your phone for work, you can add gas and cell phone expenses to Essential Expenses, and under Entertainment and Leisure you can list expenses related to your hobbies, such as photography equipment, a bicycle, and so on.

At the end of the week, add up the amounts in each subcatagory to calculate the totals for **weekly expenses** by category. Breaking down expenses by category is very useful, because it helps you understand your spending habits and assess how they affect your weekly and monthly standing.

Add up all the daily totals to assess your **weekly total**.

draw up a balance sheet at the end of the month

In the chart, record **weekly totals** and the **monthly total for each category** (Essential Expenses, Optional Expenses, Entertainment and Leisure, Extras and Unforeseen Events). This allows you to monitor your spending habit and be aware of any waste so you can target cuts or investments as needed.

Write down what you spent on **utilities** (electricity, gas, phone/Internet) here.

In the **significant expenses boxes**, write the total for any substantial expenditures (e.g., cigarettes, gas, transportation, travel) drawing on those listed in the four main categories.

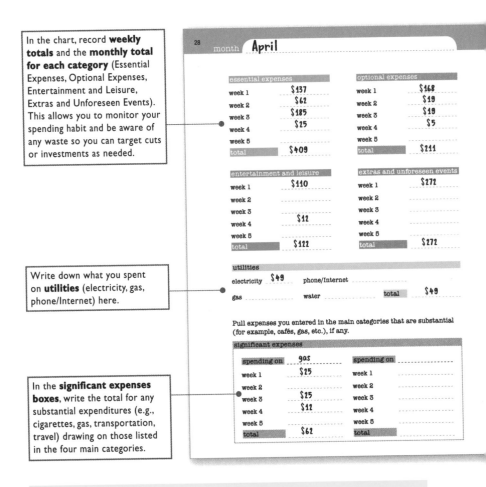

28 month **April**

essential expenses

week 1	$137
week 2	$62
week 3	$185
week 4	$25
week 5	
total	$409

optional expenses

week 1	$168
week 2	$19
week 3	$19
week 4	$5
week 5	
total	$211

entertainment and leisure

week 1	$110
week 2	
week 3	
week 4	$12
week 5	
total	$122

extras and unforeseen events

week 1	$272
week 2	
week 3	
week 4	
week 5	
total	$272

utilities

electricity $49   phone/Internet ....

gas ....   water ....   total $49

Pull expenses you entered in the main categories that are substantial (for example, cafés, gas, etc.), if any.

significant expenses

spending on	gas	spending on	
week 1	$25	week 1	
week 2		week 2	
week 3	$25	week 3	
week 4	$12	week 4	
week 5		week 5	
total	$62	total	

Tip
If a week **falls in two different months**, count it entirely in the first or second month. (For example, if the last day of February is a Tuesday, count the whole week as the first week in March). This will allow you to calculate weekly spending more precisely, and that will make your monthly and annual figures more useful.

Compare the totals in all the charts and draw **conclusions**.
For example, you may notice that you spend more than you
need to on public transit when you could save by purchasing
a weekly or monthly pass, or it might be a good idea to cut
some optional expenses.

summary of monthly expenses
29

• Compare the totals for all the charts: Which expense categories had
the greatest impact this month? Did you expect that?

- -

• Are there expenses you could cut?

- -

Write down the **total** expenses
for **each week** of the month.

weekly spending		
week 1	$686	
week 2	$81	
week 3	$204	
week 4	$42	
week 5		
utilities	$49	
total monthly spending	$1,062	

Write down the total spent on
utilities.

Add up the **weekly totals**
to determine **total monthly
spending**.

How much cash did you have available? ___ $1,159

How much did you spend? $1,062

How much did you save? ___ $97

Check the **budget** you
calculated at the beginning of
the month and write it here.

Enter your **monthly spending
total** here.

• Did you reach your goals? (☺) Yes (☹) No (X) Almost

• If yes, good job! Give yourself a small reward, but don't cancel out
all your hard work: choose something that's not too expensive but still
makes you happy. (See pages 12–15 for suggestions.)

• If no, what went wrong? What could you do next month to improve?

- -

The difference between the
budget you created at the
start of the month and your
total monthly expenses is your
savings for the month (ninety-
seven dollars in the example).

Try to set
aside your
MONTHLY SAVINGS.
You'll be very pleased
when you see how much
you can set aside
in a single year.

Reread the **goals** you set for yourself and consider the results.
Don't get discouraged if things didn't go exactly as planned. The
important thing is not to cheat, but to look at your expenses in
order to identify the strengths of your budget and consider any
missteps so you can do better the following month.

tips and tricks

Here are some suggestions that may help you get started with your kakebo: simple rules to get organized and reach your goals, tricks for saving, and some ideas that will keep you motivated and reward you occasionally.

LEGEND

get organized   **save**   **get motivated**

SET GOALS

In order to start saving, you need to set clear, specific, feasible goals, as well as a reasonable period of time to reach them.

Some examples: Deposit 5 percent of every paycheck in a savings account. Save 50 dollars per month in an emergency fund. Pay off credit card debt from the last 12 months. Save 2,000 dollars per year for a vacation or a special gift.

DON'T COUNT ON A WINDFALL

Don't take into account potential (uncertain) sources of income such as end-of-year bonuses, inheritance, or tax refunds. Your budget should include only money that you are certain to earn.

USE AN OLD-FASHIONED PIGGY BANK

Save your change in a jar or piggy bank, and don't open it until it's full. You'll be surprised what you can save this way: small change adds up.

ALWAYS WRITE A LIST BEFORE YOU GO SHOPPING

Planning is the basis for saving. Never enter a store unless you know what you need to buy. This is especially important when grocery shopping. At home, take inventory and see what you need, then stick to the list. Don't give in to the temptation to buy things you don't need.

THE TEN-SECOND RULE

Any time you're about to put something in your shopping cart that's not on your list, stop for ten seconds and ask yourself why you're buying it. If you can't come up with a good answer, put it back on the shelf. You'll stop making impulse buys if you follow this rule.

THE THIRTY-DAY RULE

Every time you're tempted to buy something and you don't know whether it will be useful, think about what you want and then wait thirty days and ask yourself if that purchase is still important to you. Most of the time your desire for it will fade, and you'll be glad you saved the money.

LIMIT EXTRAS

Limiting extra expenses may not be fun, but it is the best way to stick to your budget. If you usually stay in a hotel when you go on vacation, this year try renting an apartment or vacationing close to home. If you like getting a massage or getting your hair done once a week, try cutting back to once a month. If you love eating in restaurants, do your best to limit those meals to once a week.

TRY TO CUT BACK ON FIXED EXPENSES

Consider ways to cut your fixed expenses—such as changing to a less costly cell phone plan or cutting channels from your television package. You can also save by making your home more energy efficient.

GET THE BEST BANK ACCOUNT FOR YOU

Don't spend your hard-earned money on bank fees and charges. Take a look at your online account. Also, if you earn little or no interest, look at savings accounts and certificates of deposit. They might provide better risk-free ways to accrue interest.

useful ideas

CARPOOLING

Do you know someone who takes the same route to work that you do? Why not share the ride, alternating days? That will cut your gas costs in half and you'll see results immediately. The savings in a single month can be significant.

PAY OFF YOUR CREDIT CARD EVERY MONTH

If you use credit cards, be sure to pay your bill in full each month—the interest and fees add up very quickly. If you can't pay off the amount you owe, make it a priority to do so in a reasonable amount of time so that you'll be debt-free.

PAY CASH AND KEEP YOUR RECEIPTS

It's better to pay for most of your daily expenses in cash, especially when it comes to extras at cafés, restaurants, and convenience stores. When you pay cash, you're more aware of what you spend. Keep all your receipts and record your expenses in your kakebo each night.

SAVE ENERGY

Here are some tips for keeping your electric bill low: only run your washing machine and dishwasher when they're full. Set your water temperature to 104 degrees [40 degrees Celsius] and clean the filters and baskets. Turn off your TV and other electronics when not in use. Watch TV in low light and turn off lights when you don't need them. To save on home heating bills, have your heating system checked annually. Set the thermostat to 68 degrees [20 degrees Celsius]. Turn off the heat an hour before you go to bed, and turn off radiators when you don't need them. Take a shower rather than a bath and shut off the water while you're soaping up, then turn it back on to rinse off.

DON'T SPEND MONEY TO COMBAT STRESS

Many people spend money as a way to relax after a stressful day at work—compulsive shopping, video games, junk food, scratch-off lottery tickets, etc. But the best way to relax is to take a few moments for yourself: take a walk, listen to music, or just lie on the couch and breathe deeply.

TALK TO YOUR LOVED ONES ABOUT YOUR PLANS

This might sound like a strange way to save money, but it works. Spending time with the people you love most and turning to them for moral support as you try to reach your goals will make it easier for you to organize your steps and stick to your plan.

REWARD YOURSELF EVERY ONCE IN A WHILE—WITHIN REASON

Use your money; don't let your money use you. You shouldn't feel shackled to a budget or restricted by money at all times. Give yourself a small reward every once in a while. Don't waste your savings on expensive products and services, but do allow yourself the occasional small treat—a pastry in a café, a new sweater, or a gift for a loved one.

DON'T BE AFRAID TO SAY NO

If your friends ask you to go out but you don't want to spend money, don't be afraid to say no. Or try inviting them to dinner at your house—you'll save money and you'll have a chance to cook and care for people you love. In return, you'll enjoy their gratitude and their company.

DON'T BEAT YOURSELF UP WHEN YOU MAKE A MISTAKE

We all tend to regret our bad choices, even when they're offset by so many more good ones. If you make a mistake (a bad investment, an unwise purchase), the important thing is to learn from it. If you understand why you did it, you run less risk of repeating it in the future.

LOOK TO THE FUTURE

The choices you make now won't change the past, but they will definitely change the future. There's always room for improvement. Just keep trying!

NEVER GIVE UP

If you feel like you're drowning in expenses, talk about it with your loved ones and consult a financial consultant or consumer affairs group. Remember that many people are fighting the same battle. You're not alone.

month

_____

record your monthly income and spending

income

date	item	amount
-----------	-----------------------	-------------------
-----------	-----------------------	-------------------
-----------	-----------------------	-------------------
-----------	-----------------------	-------------------
-----------	-----------------------	-------------------
-----------	-----------------------	-------------------
-----------	-----------------------	-------------------
-----------	-----------------------	-------------------
total income		-------------------

fixed expenses

rent/ mortgage	----------------	maintenance/ HOA fees	----------------
bus/subway pass	----------------	parking space	----------------
school/ cafeteria	----------------	gym	----------------
social insurance contributions	----------------	self-employment tax	----------------
	----------------		----------------
	----------------		----------------
	----------------		----------------
	----------------		----------------
total fixed expenses			----------------

goals and forecast

- **Which expenses do you plan to cut to save money?**

- **How can you reach your goals?**

How much do you
want to save?

_____

How much money do you have available
this month?

income	fixed expenses	forecast savings
_____	_____	_____

cash
available

=
_____

	Monday	Tuesday	Wednesday	Thursday
essential expenses				
optional expenses				
entertainment and leisure				
extras and unforeseen events				
total				

Friday	Saturday	Sunday	weekly expenses

essential expenses

supermarket ....

other food ....

pharmacy ....

transportation ....

children ....

pets ....

....

....

....

total ....

optional expenses

shopping ....

cosmetics ....

gifts ....

....

....

total ....

entertainment and leisure

books & magazines ....

music ....

movies and shows ....

cafés and takeout ....

restaurants ....

....

total ....

extras and unforeseen events

medical expenses ....

travel ....

....

....

total ....

weekly
total

month ....

	Monday..........	Tuesday..........	Wednesday.....	Thursday........
essential expenses				
optional expenses				
entertainment and leisure				
extras and unforeseen events				
total				

Friday_____	Saturday_____	Sunday_____

weekly expenses

essential expenses

supermarket	_____
other food	_____
pharmacy	_____
transportation	_____
children	_____
pets	_____
_____	_____
_____	_____
_____	_____
total	_____

optional expenses

shopping	_____
cosmetics	_____
gifts	_____
_____	_____
_____	_____
total	_____

entertainment and leisure

books & magazines	_____
music	_____
movies and shows	_____
cafés and takeout	_____
restaurants	_____
_____	_____
total	_____

extras and unforeseen events

medical expenses	_____
travel	_____
_____	_____
_____	_____
total	_____

weekly total	_____

	Monday	Tuesday	Wednesday	Thursday
essential expenses				
optional expenses				
entertainment and leisure				
extras and unforeseen events				
total				

Friday_____	Saturday_____	Sunday_____

weekly expenses

essential expenses

supermarket	
other food	
pharmacy	
transportation	
children	
pets	
total	

optional expenses

shopping	
cosmetics	
gifts	
total	

entertainment and leisure

books & magazines	
music	
movies and shows	
cafés and takeout	
restaurants	
total	

extras and unforeseen events

medical expenses	
travel	
total	

weekly total	

month ----------------------------------

	Monday.........	Tuesday.........	Wednesday......	Thursday.......
essential expenses				
optional expenses				
entertainment and leisure				
extras and unforeseen events				
total				

Friday	Saturday	Sunday

weekly expenses

essential expenses

supermarket	
other food	
pharmacy	
transportation	
children	
pets	
total	

optional expenses

shopping	
cosmetics	
gifts	
total	

entertainment and leisure

books & magazines	
music	
movies and shows	
cafés and takeout	
restaurants	
total	

extras and unforeseen events

medical expenses	
travel	
total	

| **weekly total** | |

	Monday	Tuesday	Wednesday	Thursday
essential expenses				
optional expenses				
entertainment and leisure				
extras and unforeseen events				
total				

Friday	Saturday	Sunday	weekly expenses

weekly expenses

essential expenses

supermarket	
other food	
pharmacy	
transportation	
children	
pets	
total	

optional expenses

shopping	
cosmetics	
gifts	
total	

entertainment and leisure

books & magazines	
music	
movies and shows	
cafés and takeout	
restaurants	
total	

extras and unforeseen events

medical expenses	
travel	
total	

weekly total	

essential expenses

week 1 ....
week 2 ....
week 3 ....
week 4 ....
week 5 ....
total ....

optional expenses

week 1 ....
week 2 ....
week 3 ....
week 4 ....
week 5 ....
total ....

entertainment and leisure

week 1 ....
week 2 ....
week 3 ....
week 4 ....
week 5 ....
total ....

extras and unforeseen events

week 1 ....
week 2 ....
week 3 ....
week 4 ....
week 5 ....
total ....

utilities

electricity ....   phone/Internet ....

gas ....   water ....   **total** ....

Pull expenses you entered in the main categories that are substantial
(for example, cafés, gas, etc.), if any.

significant expenses

spending on ....   **spending on** ....

week 1 ....   week 1 ....
week 2 ....   week 2 ....
week 3 ....   week 3 ....
week 4 ....   week 4 ....
week 5 ....   week 5 ....
total ....   **total** ....

29

summary of monthly expenses

- Compare the totals for all the charts: Which expense categories had the greatest impact this month? Did you expect that?

- -

- Are there expenses you could cut?

- -

weekly spending

week 1	- - - - - - - - - -
week 2	- - - - - - - - - -
week 3	- - - - - - - - - -
week 4	- - - - - - - - - -
week 5	- - - - - - - - - -
utilities	- - - - - - - - - -
total monthly spending	- - - - - - - - - -

How much cash did you have available? - - - - - - - - - - - - - - - -

How much did you spend? - - - - - - - - - - - - -

How much did you save? - - - - - - - - - - - - - - -

- Did you reach your goals?　　🙂 Yes　　🙁 No　　😐 Almost

- If yes, good job! Give yourself a small reward, but don't cancel out all your hard work: choose something that's not too expensive but still makes you happy.

- If no, what went wrong? What could you do next month to improve?

- -
- -
- -
- -

month

record your monthly income and spending

income

date	item	amount
total income		

fixed expenses

rent/ mortgage		maintenance/ HOA fees	
bus/subway pass		parking space	
school/ cafeteria		gym	
social insurance contributions		self-employment tax	
total fixed expenses			

goals and forecast

- Which expenses do you plan to cut to save money?

_____

_____

- How can you reach your goals?

_____

_____

_____

How much do you
want to save?

_____

How much money do you have available
this month?

income		fixed expenses		forecast savings
_____	−	_____	−	_____

cash
available

=

_____

	Monday	Tuesday	Wednesday	Thursday
essential expenses				
optional expenses				
entertainment and leisure				
extras and unforeseen events				
total				

Friday	Saturday	Sunday

weekly expenses

essential expenses

supermarket

other food

pharmacy

transportation

children

pets

total

optional expenses

shopping

cosmetics

gifts

total

entertainment and leisure

books & magazines

music

movies and shows

cafés and takeout

restaurants

total

extras and unforeseen events

medical expenses

travel

total

weekly total

month _____

	Monday_____	Tuesday_____	Wednesday_____	Thursday_____
essential expenses				
optional expenses				
entertainment and leisure				
extras and unforeseen events				
total				

Friday	Saturday	Sunday	weekly expenses

weekly expenses

essential expenses

supermarket	
other food	
pharmacy	
transportation	
children	
pets	
total	

optional expenses

shopping	
cosmetics	
gifts	
total	

entertainment and leisure

books & magazines	
music	
movies and shows	
cafés and takeout	
restaurants	
total	

extras and unforeseen events

medical expenses	
travel	
total	

weekly total	

	Monday	Tuesday	Wednesday	Thursday
essential expenses				
optional expenses				
entertainment and leisure				
extras and unforeseen events				
total				

Friday	Saturday	Sunday

weekly expenses

essential expenses

supermarket

other food

pharmacy

transportation

children

pets

total

optional expenses

shopping

cosmetics

gifts

total

entertainment and leisure

books & magazines

music

movies and shows

cafés and takeout

restaurants

total

extras and unforeseen events

medical expenses

travel

total

weekly total

month _____

	Monday	Tuesday	Wednesday	Thursday
essential expenses				
optional expenses				
entertainment and leisure				
extras and unforeseen events				
total				

Friday_____ Saturday_____ Sunday_____

weekly expenses

essential expenses

supermarket	
other food	
pharmacy	
transportation	
children	
pets	
total	

optional expenses

shopping	
cosmetics	
gifts	
total	

entertainment and leisure

books & magazines	
music	
movies and shows	
cafés and takeout	
restaurants	
total	

extras and unforeseen events

medical expenses	
travel	
total	

weekly total

month _____

	Monday _____	Tuesday _____	Wednesday _____	Thursday _____
essential expenses				
optional expenses				
entertainment and leisure				
extras and unforeseen events				
total				

Friday_____	Saturday_____	Sunday_____

weekly expenses

essential expenses

supermarket _____

other food _____

pharmacy _____

transportation _____

children _____

pets _____

_____ _____

_____ _____

_____ _____

total _____

optional expenses

shopping _____

cosmetics _____

gifts _____

_____ _____

_____ _____

total _____

entertainment and leisure

books & magazines _____

music _____

movies and shows _____

cafés and takeout _____

restaurants _____

_____ _____

total _____

extras and unforeseen events

medical expenses _____

travel _____

_____ _____

_____ _____

total _____

weekly total _____

essential expenses

week 1 ....
week 2 ....
week 3 ....
week 4 ....
week 5 ....
total ....

optional expenses

week 1 ....
week 2 ....
week 3 ....
week 4 ....
week 5 ....
total ....

entertainment and leisure

week 1 ....
week 2 ....
week 3 ....
week 4 ....
week 5 ....
total ....

extras and unforeseen events

week 1 ....
week 2 ....
week 3 ....
week 4 ....
week 5 ....
total ....

utilities

electricity ....   phone/Internet ....

gas ....   water ....   total ....

Pull expenses you entered in the main categories that are substantial (for example, cafés, gas, etc.), if any.

significant expenses

spending on ....   spending on ....

week 1 ....   week 1 ....
week 2 ....   week 2 ....
week 3 ....   week 3 ....
week 4 ....   week 4 ....
week 5 ....   week 5 ....
total ....   total ....

- Compare the totals for all the charts: Which expense categories had the greatest impact this month? Did you expect that?

- -

- Are there expenses you could cut?

- -

weekly spending

week 1	- - - - - - - - - - -
week 2	- - - - - - - - - - -
week 3	- - - - - - - - - - -
week 4	- - - - - - - - - - -
week 5	- - - - - - - - - - -
utilities	- - - - - - - - - - -
total monthly spending	- - - - - - - - - - -

How much cash did you have available? - - - - - - - - - - - - - - - -

How much did you spend? - - - - - - - - - - - - - - -

How much did you save? - - - - - - - - - - - - - - - -

- Did you reach your goals?   ☺ Yes   ☹ No   😐 Almost

- If yes, good job! Give yourself a small reward, but don't cancel out all your hard work: choose something that's not too expensive but still makes you happy.

- If no, what went wrong? What could you do next month to improve?

- -
- -
- -
- -

month

_____

record your monthly income and spending

income

date	item	amount
total income		

fixed expenses

rent/ mortgage		maintenance/ HOA fees	
bus/subway pass		parking space	
school/ cafeteria		gym	
social insurance contributions		self-employment tax	
total fixed expenses			

goals and forecast

- **Which expenses do you plan to cut to save money?**

- **How can you reach your goals?**

 How much do you
want to save?

_____

How much money do you have available
this month?

income		fixed expenses		forecast savings
_____	−	_____	−	_____

=

 cash
available

_____

month --

	Monday	Tuesday	Wednesday	Thursday
essential expenses				
optional expenses				
entertainment and leisure				
extras and unforeseen events				
total				

Friday_____ Saturday_____ Sunday_____

weekly expenses

essential expenses

supermarket _____

other food _____

pharmacy _____

transportation _____

children _____

pets _____

_____ _____

_____ _____

_____ _____

total _____

optional expenses

shopping _____

cosmetics _____

gifts _____

_____ _____

_____ _____

total _____

entertainment and leisure

books & magazines _____

music _____

movies and shows _____

cafés and takeout _____

restaurants _____

_____ _____

total _____

extras and unforeseen events

medical expenses _____

travel _____

_____ _____

_____ _____

total _____

weekly total _____

month ....

	Monday........	Tuesday........	Wednesday.....	Thursday.......
essential expenses				
optional expenses				
entertainment and leisure				
extras and unforeseen events				
total				

Friday	Saturday	Sunday

weekly expenses

essential expenses

supermarket

other food

pharmacy

transportation

children

pets

- - - - - - - - - - - - - - - -

- - - - - - - - - - - - - - - -

- - - - - - - - - - - - - - - -

total

optional expenses

shopping

cosmetics

gifts

- - - - - - - - - - - - - - - -

- - - - - - - - - - - - - - - -

total

entertainment and leisure

books & magazines

music

movies and shows

cafés and takeout

restaurants

- - - - - - - - - - - - - - - -

total

extras and unforeseen events

medical expenses

travel

- - - - - - - - - - - - - - - -

- - - - - - - - - - - - - - - -

total

weekly
total

	Monday	Tuesday	Wednesday	Thursday
essential expenses				
optional expenses				
entertainment and leisure				
extras and unforeseen events				
total				

Friday_____	Saturday_____	Sunday_____	weekly expenses

essential expenses

supermarket	_____
other food	_____
pharmacy	_____
transportation	_____
children	_____
pets	_____
_____	_____
_____	_____
_____	_____
total	_____

optional expenses

shopping	_____
cosmetics	_____
gifts	_____
_____	_____
_____	_____
total	_____

entertainment and leisure

books & magazines	_____
music	_____
movies and shows	_____
cafés and takeout	_____
restaurants	_____
_____	_____
total	_____

extras and unforeseen events

medical expenses	_____
travel	_____
_____	_____
_____	_____
total	_____
weekly total	_____

	Monday	Tuesday	Wednesday	Thursday
essential expenses				
optional expenses				
entertainment and leisure				
extras and unforeseen events				
total				

Friday _____	Saturday _____	Sunday _____

weekly expenses

essential expenses

supermarket _____

other food _____

pharmacy _____

transportation _____

children _____

pets _____

_____ _____

_____ _____

_____ _____

total _____

optional expenses

shopping _____

cosmetics _____

gifts _____

_____ _____

_____ _____

total _____

entertainment and leisure

books & magazines _____

music _____

movies and shows _____

cafés and takeout _____

restaurants _____

_____ _____

total _____

extras and unforeseen events

medical expenses _____

travel _____

_____ _____

_____ _____

total _____

weekly
total _____

month ....

	Monday..........	Tuesday........	Wednesday.....	Thursday.......
essential expenses				
optional expenses				
entertainment and leisure				
extras and unforeseen events				
total				

Friday	Saturday	Sunday	weekly expenses

essential expenses

supermarket

other food

pharmacy

transportation

children

pets

total

optional expenses

shopping

cosmetics

gifts

total

entertainment and leisure

books & magazines

music

movies and shows

cafés and takeout

restaurants

total

extras and unforeseen events

medical expenses

travel

total

weekly total

essential expenses

week 1 ....
week 2 ....
week 3 ....
week 4 ....
week 5 ....
total ....

optional expenses

week 1 ....
week 2 ....
week 3 ....
week 4 ....
week 5 ....
total ....

entertainment and leisure

week 1 ....
week 2 ....
week 3 ....
week 4 ....
week 5 ....
total ....

extras and unforeseen events

week 1 ....
week 2 ....
week 3 ....
week 4 ....
week 5 ....
total ....

utilities

electricity .... phone/Internet ....

gas .... water .... total ....

Pull expenses you entered in the main categories that are substantial (for example, cafés, gas, etc.), if any.

significant expenses

spending on .... spending on ....

week 1 ....
week 2 ....
week 3 ....
week 4 ....
week 5 ....
total ....

week 1 ....
week 2 ....
week 3 ....
week 4 ....
week 5 ....
total ....

summary of monthly expenses

- Compare the totals for all the charts: Which expense categories had the greatest impact this month? Did you expect that?

- -

- Are there expenses you could cut?

- -

weekly spending

week 1	- - - - - - - - - -
week 2	- - - - - - - - - -
week 3	- - - - - - - - - -
week 4	- - - - - - - - - -
week 5	- - - - - - - - - -
utilities	- - - - - - - - - -
total monthly spending	- - - - - - - - - -

How much cash did you have available? - - - - - - - - - - - - - - -

How much did you spend? - - - - - - - - - - - - -

How much did you save? - - - - - - - - - - - - - - - - - -

- Did you reach your goals?   😊 Yes   ☹️ No   😐 Almost

- If yes, good job! Give yourself a small reward, but don't cancel out all your hard work: choose something that's not too expensive but still makes you happy.

- If no, what went wrong? What could you do next month to improve?

- -
- -
- -
- -

month

_____

record your monthly income and spending

income

date	item	amount

total income	

fixed expenses

rent/ mortgage		maintenance/ HOA fees	
bus/subway pass		parking space	
school/ cafeteria		gym	
social insurance contributions		self-employment tax	

total fixed expenses	

goals and forecast

- Which expenses do you plan to cut to save money?

- -

- -

- How can you reach your goals?

- -

- -

- -

How much do you want to save?

How much money do you have available this month?

income − fixed expenses − forecast savings

= cash available

month ....

	Monday..........	Tuesday........	Wednesday.....	Thursday.......
essential expenses				
optional expenses				
entertainment and leisure				
extras and unforeseen events				
total				

Friday	Saturday	Sunday

weekly expenses

essential expenses

supermarket

other food

pharmacy

transportation

children

pets

total

optional expenses

shopping

cosmetics

gifts

total

entertainment and leisure

books & magazines

music

movies and shows

cafés and takeout

restaurants

total

extras and unforeseen events

medical expenses

travel

total

weekly total

month

	Monday	Tuesday	Wednesday	Thursday
essential expenses				
optional expenses				
entertainment and leisure				
extras and unforeseen events				
total				

Friday	Saturday	Sunday

weekly expenses

essential expenses

supermarket

other food

pharmacy

transportation

children

pets

total

optional expenses

shopping

cosmetics

gifts

total

entertainment and leisure

books & magazines

music

movies and shows

cafés and takeout

restaurants

total

extras and unforeseen events

medical expenses

travel

total

weekly total

month

	Monday	Tuesday	Wednesday	Thursday
essential expenses				
optional expenses				
entertainment and leisure				
extras and unforeseen events				
total				

Friday	Saturday	Sunday	weekly expenses

weekly expenses

essential expenses

supermarket	_____
other food	_____
pharmacy	_____
transportation	_____
children	_____
pets	_____
_____	_____
_____	_____
_____	_____
total	_____

optional expenses

shopping	_____
cosmetics	_____
gifts	_____
_____	_____
_____	_____
total	_____

entertainment and leisure

books & magazines	_____
music	_____
movies and shows	_____
cafés and takeout	_____
restaurants	_____
_____	_____
total	_____

extras and unforeseen events

medical expenses	_____
travel	_____
_____	_____
_____	_____
total	_____
weekly total	_____

	Monday...........	Tuesday.........	Wednesday......	Thursday........
essential expenses				
optional expenses				
entertainment and leisure				
extras and unforeseen events				
total				

Friday..........	Saturday.......	Sunday.........

weekly expenses

essential expenses

supermarket	....
other food	....
pharmacy	....
transportation	....
children	....
pets	....
....	....
....	....
....	....

total	....

optional expenses

shopping	....
cosmetics	....
gifts	....
....	....
....	....

total	....

entertainment and leisure

books & magazines	....
music	....
movies and shows	....
cafés and takeout	....
restaurants	....
....	....

total	....

extras and unforeseen events

medical expenses	....
travel	....
....	....
....	....

total	....

weekly total	

	Monday	Tuesday	Wednesday	Thursday
essential expenses				
optional expenses				
entertainment and leisure				
extras and unforeseen events				
total				

Friday..........	Saturday.......	Sunday..........

weekly expenses

essential expenses

supermarket ....

other food ....

pharmacy ....

transportation ....

children ....

pets ....

....

....

....

total ....

optional expenses

shopping ....

cosmetics ....

gifts ....

....

....

total ....

entertainment and leisure

books & magazines ....

music ....

movies and shows ....

cafés and takeout ....

restaurants ....

....

total ....

extras and unforeseen events

medical expenses ....

travel ....

....

....

total ....

weekly total ....

essential expenses

week 1 ....
week 2 ....
week 3 ....
week 4 ....
week 5 ....
total ....

optional expenses

week 1 ....
week 2 ....
week 3 ....
week 4 ....
week 5 ....
total ....

entertainment and leisure

week 1 ....
week 2 ....
week 3 ....
week 4 ....
week 5 ....
total ....

extras and unforeseen events

week 1 ....
week 2 ....
week 3 ....
week 4 ....
week 5 ....
total ....

utilities

electricity .... phone/Internet ....

gas .... water .... total ....

Pull expenses you entered in the main categories that are substantial (for example, cafés, gas, etc.), if any.

significant expenses

spending on .... spending on ....

week 1 .... week 1 ....
week 2 .... week 2 ....
week 3 .... week 3 ....
week 4 .... week 4 ....
week 5 .... week 5 ....
total .... total ....

summary of monthly expenses

- Compare the totals for all the charts: Which expense categories had the greatest impact this month? Did you expect that?

- -

- Are there expenses you could cut?

- -

weekly spending

week 1	- - - - - - - - -
week 2	- - - - - - - - -
week 3	- - - - - - - - -
week 4	- - - - - - - - -
week 5	- - - - - - - - -
utilities	- - - - - - - - -
total monthly spending	- - - - - - - - -

How much cash did you have available? - - - - - - - - - - - - - -

How much did you spend? - - - - - - - - - -

How much did you save? - - - - - - - - - - - - -

- Did you reach your goals? ☺ Yes   ☹ No   😐 Almost

- If yes, good job! Give yourself a small reward, but don't cancel out all your hard work: choose something that's not too expensive but still makes you happy.

- If no, what went wrong? What could you do next month to improve?

- -
- -
- -
- -

month

_____

record your monthly income and spending

income

date	item	amount
total income		

fixed expenses

rent/ mortgage		maintenance/ HOA fees	
bus/subway pass		parking space	
school/ cafeteria		gym	
social insurance contributions		self-employment tax	
total fixed expenses			

goals and forecast

- Which expenses do you plan to cut to save money?

- How can you reach your goals?

 How much do you want to save?

_____

How much money do you have available this month?

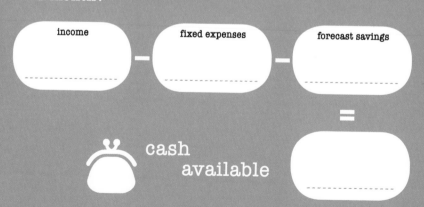

income	fixed expenses	forecast savings
_____	_____	_____

income − fixed expenses − forecast savings

cash available =

_____

month ------------------------------

	Monday........	Tuesday........	Wednesday.....	Thursday.......
essential expenses				
optional expenses				
entertainment and leisure				
extras and unforeseen events				
total				

Friday	Saturday	Sunday

weekly expenses

essential expenses

supermarket	
other food	
pharmacy	
transportation	
children	
pets	
total	

optional expenses

shopping	
cosmetics	
gifts	
total	

entertainment and leisure

books & magazines	
music	
movies and shows	
cafés and takeout	
restaurants	
total	

extras and unforeseen events

medical expenses	
travel	
total	

weekly total	

month ....

	Monday.........	Tuesday.........	Wednesday.....	Thursday........
essential expenses				
optional expenses				
entertainment and leisure				
extras and unforeseen events				
total				

Friday	Saturday	Sunday

weekly expenses

essential expenses

supermarket	
other food	
pharmacy	
transportation	
children	
pets	
total	

optional expenses

shopping	
cosmetics	
gifts	
total	

entertainment and leisure

books & magazines	
music	
movies and shows	
cafés and takeout	
restaurants	
total	

extras and unforeseen events

medical expenses	
travel	
total	

weekly total	

month ....

	Monday.........	Tuesday........	Wednesday.....	Thursday.......
essential expenses				
optional expenses				
entertainment and leisure				
extras and unforeseen events				
total				

Friday	Saturday	Sunday	weekly expenses

essential expenses

supermarket	
other food	
pharmacy	
transportation	
children	
pets	
total	

optional expenses

shopping	
cosmetics	
gifts	
total	

entertainment and leisure

books & magazines	
music	
movies and shows	
cafés and takeout	
restaurants	
total	

extras and unforeseen events

medical expenses	
travel	
total	

weekly total	

month

	Monday	Tuesday	Wednesday	Thursday
essential expenses				
optional expenses				
entertainment and leisure				
extras and unforeseen events				
total				

Friday	Saturday	Sunday	weekly expenses

essential expenses

supermarket

other food

pharmacy

transportation

children

pets

total

optional expenses

shopping

cosmetics

gifts

total

entertainment and leisure

books & magazines

music

movies and shows

cafés and takeout

restaurants

total

extras and unforeseen events

medical expenses

travel

total

weekly total

	Monday	Tuesday	Wednesday	Thursday
essential expenses				
optional expenses				
entertainment and leisure				
extras and unforeseen events				
total				

Friday	Saturday	Sunday	weekly expenses

weekly expenses

essential expenses

supermarket	
other food	
pharmacy	
transportation	
children	
pets	
total	

optional expenses

shopping	
cosmetics	
gifts	
total	

entertainment and leisure

books & magazines	
music	
movies and shows	
cafés and takeout	
restaurants	
total	

extras and unforeseen events

medical expenses	
travel	
total	

weekly total	

essential expenses

week 1 ....
week 2 ....
week 3 ....
week 4 ....
week 5 ....
total ....

optional expenses

week 1 ....
week 2 ....
week 3 ....
week 4 ....
week 5 ....
total ....

entertainment and leisure

week 1 ....
week 2 ....
week 3 ....
week 4 ....
week 5 ....
total ....

extras and unforeseen events

week 1 ....
week 2 ....
week 3 ....
week 4 ....
week 5 ....
total ....

utilities

electricity .... phone/Internet ....

gas .... water .... total ....

Pull expenses you entered in the main categories that are substantial (for example, cafés, gas, etc.), if any.

significant expenses

spending on .... spending on ....

week 1 ....
week 2 ....
week 3 ....
week 4 ....
week 5 ....
total ....

week 1 ....
week 2 ....
week 3 ....
week 4 ....
week 5 ....
total ....

summary of monthly expenses

- Compare the totals for all the charts: Which expense categories had the greatest impact this month? Did you expect that?

- Are there expenses you could cut?

----

weekly spending

week 1	_____
week 2	_____
week 3	_____
week 4	_____
week 5	_____
utilities	_____
total monthly spending	_____

How much cash did you have available? _____

How much did you spend? _____

How much did you save? _____

- Did you reach your goals? ☺ Yes ☹ No 😐 Almost

- If yes, good job! Give yourself a small reward, but don't cancel out all your hard work: choose something that's not too expensive but still makes you happy.

- If no, what went wrong? What could you do next month to improve?

----

month

record your monthly income and spending

income

date	item	amount
total income		

fixed expenses

rent/ mortgage		maintenance/ HOA fees	
bus/subway pass		parking space	
school/ cafeteria		gym	
social insurance contributions		self-employment tax	
total fixed expenses			

goals and forecast

- Which expenses do you plan to cut to save money?

_____

_____

- How can you reach your goals?

_____

_____

_____

How much do you
want to save?

_____

How much money do you have available
this month?

income	fixed expenses	forecast savings
_____	_____	_____

− −

=

cash
available

_____

month

	Monday	Tuesday	Wednesday	Thursday
essential expenses				
optional expenses				
entertainment and leisure				
extras and unforeseen events				
total				

Friday	Saturday	Sunday

weekly expenses

essential expenses

supermarket _____
other food _____
pharmacy _____
transportation _____
children _____
pets _____
_____ _____
_____ _____
_____ _____

total _____

optional expenses

shopping _____
cosmetics _____
gifts _____
_____ _____
_____ _____

total _____

entertainment and leisure

books & magazines _____
music _____
movies and shows _____
cafés and takeout _____
restaurants _____
_____ _____

total _____

extras and unforeseen events

medical expenses _____
travel _____
_____ _____
_____ _____

total _____

weekly total _____

	Monday	Tuesday	Wednesday	Thursday
essential expenses				
optional expenses				
entertainment and leisure				
extras and unforeseen events				
total				

Friday	Saturday	Sunday

weekly expenses

essential expenses

supermarket	
other food	
pharmacy	
transportation	
children	
pets	
total	

optional expenses

shopping	
cosmetics	
gifts	
total	

entertainment and leisure

books & magazines	
music	
movies and shows	
cafés and takeout	
restaurants	
total	

extras and unforeseen events

medical expenses	
travel	
total	

weekly total	

month

	Monday	Tuesday	Wednesday	Thursday
essential expenses				
optional expenses				
entertainment and leisure				
extras and unforeseen events				
total				

Friday	Saturday	Sunday	weekly expenses

essential expenses

supermarket

other food

pharmacy

transportation

children

pets

total

optional expenses

shopping

cosmetics

gifts

total

entertainment and leisure

books & magazines

music

movies and shows

cafés and takeout

restaurants

total

extras and unforeseen events

medical expenses

travel

total

weekly total

	Monday	Tuesday	Wednesday	Thursday
essential expenses				
optional expenses				
entertainment and leisure				
extras and unforeseen events				
total				

Friday	Saturday	Sunday

weekly expenses

essential expenses

supermarket

other food

pharmacy

transportation

children

pets

total

optional expenses

shopping

cosmetics

gifts

total

entertainment and leisure

books & magazines

music

movies and shows

cafés and takeout

restaurants

total

extras and unforeseen events

medical expenses

travel

total

weekly total

month ....

	Monday..........	Tuesday..........	Wednesday......	Thursday........
essential expenses				
optional expenses				
entertainment and leisure				
extras and unforeseen events				
total				

Friday	Saturday	Sunday	weekly expenses

essential expenses

supermarket	
other food	
pharmacy	
transportation	
children	
pets	

total

optional expenses

shopping	
cosmetics	
gifts	

total

entertainment and leisure

books & magazines	
music	
movies and shows	
cafés and takeout	
restaurants	

total

extras and unforeseen events

| medical expenses | |
| travel | |

total

weekly total

month

essential expenses

week 1 ....
week 2 ....
week 3 ....
week 4 ....
week 5 ....
total ....

optional expenses

week 1 ....
week 2 ....
week 3 ....
week 4 ....
week 5 ....
total ....

entertainment and leisure

week 1 ....
week 2 ....
week 3 ....
week 4 ....
week 5 ....
total ....

extras and unforeseen events

week 1 ....
week 2 ....
week 3 ....
week 4 ....
week 5 ....
total ....

utilities

electricity .... phone/Internet ....

gas .... water .... total ....

Pull expenses you entered in the main categories that are substantial
(for example, cafés, gas, etc.), if any.

significant expenses

spending on .... spending on ....

week 1 .... week 1 ....
week 2 .... week 2 ....
week 3 .... week 3 ....
week 4 .... week 4 ....
week 5 .... week 5 ....
total .... total ....

summary of monthly expenses

- Compare the totals for all the charts: Which expense categories had the greatest impact this month? Did you expect that?

- -

- Are there expenses you could cut?

- -

weekly spending

week 1	- - - - - - - - - - - -
week 2	- - - - - - - - - - - -
week 3	- - - - - - - - - - - -
week 4	- - - - - - - - - - - -
week 5	- - - - - - - - - - - -
utilities	- - - - - - - - - - - -
total monthly spending	- - - - - - - - - - - -

How much cash did you have available? - - - - - - - - - - - - - - - -

How much did you spend? - - - - - - - - - - - - -

How much did you save? - - - - - - - - - - - - - - -

- Did you reach your goals? ☺ Yes   ☹ No   😐 Almost

- If yes, good job! Give yourself a small reward, but don't cancel out all your hard work: choose something that's not too expensive but still makes you happy.

- If no, what went wrong? What could you do next month to improve?

- -
- -
- -
- -

month

_____

record your monthly income and spending

income

date	item	amount
-----	-----	-----
-----	-----	-----
-----	-----	-----
-----	-----	-----
-----	-----	-----
-----	-----	-----
-----	-----	-----
-----	-----	-----

total income	
	-----

fixed expenses

rent/ mortgage	-----	maintenance/ HOA fees	-----
bus/subway pass	-----	parking space	-----
school/ cafeteria	-----	gym	-----
social insurance contributions	-----	self-employment tax	-----
	-----		-----
	-----		-----
	-----		-----
	-----		-----

total fixed expenses	
	-----

goals and forecast

- Which expenses do you plan to cut to save money?

_____

_____

- How can you reach your goals?

_____

_____

_____

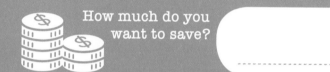

How much do you
want to save?

_____

How much money do you have available
this month?

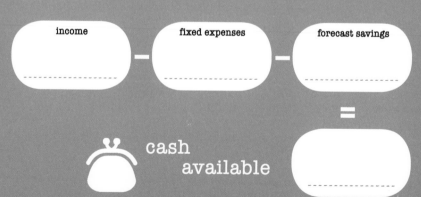

income	fixed expenses	forecast savings
_____	_____	_____

cash
available

=

_____

month

	Monday	Tuesday	Wednesday	Thursday
essential expenses				
optional expenses				
entertainment and leisure				
extras and unforeseen events				
total				

Friday	Saturday	Sunday

weekly expenses

essential expenses

supermarket	
other food	
pharmacy	
transportation	
children	
pets	
total	

optional expenses

shopping	
cosmetics	
gifts	
total	

entertainment and leisure

books & magazines	
music	
movies and shows	
cafés and takeout	
restaurants	
total	

extras and unforeseen events

medical expenses	
travel	
total	

weekly total	

month ....

	Monday..........	Tuesday.........	Wednesday.....	Thursday.......
essential expenses				
optional expenses				
entertainment and leisure				
extras and unforeseen events				
total				

Friday	Saturday	Sunday

weekly expenses

essential expenses

supermarket

other food

pharmacy

transportation

children

pets

total

optional expenses

shopping

cosmetics

gifts

total

entertainment and leisure

books & magazines

music

movies and shows

cafés and takeout

restaurants

total

extras and unforeseen events

medical expenses

travel

total

weekly total

month ---------------------------------

	Monday.........	Tuesday.........	Wednesday.....	Thursday.......
essential expenses				
optional expenses				
entertainment and leisure				
extras and unforeseen events				
total				

Friday	Saturday	Sunday	weekly expenses

essential expenses

supermarket

other food

pharmacy

transportation

children

pets

total

optional expenses

shopping

cosmetics

gifts

total

entertainment and leisure

books & magazines

music

movies and shows

cafés and takeout

restaurants

total

extras and unforeseen events

medical expenses

travel

total

weekly total

month

	Monday	Tuesday	Wednesday	Thursday
essential expenses				
optional expenses				
entertainment and leisure				
extras and unforeseen events				
total				

Friday	Saturday	Sunday

weekly expenses

essential expenses

supermarket

other food

pharmacy

transportation

children

pets

total

optional expenses

shopping

cosmetics

gifts

total

entertainment and leisure

books & magazines

music

movies and shows

cafés and takeout

restaurants

total

extras and unforeseen events

medical expenses

travel

total

weekly total

month ....

	Monday..........	Tuesday..........	Wednesday......	Thursday........
essential expenses				
optional expenses				
entertainment and leisure				
extras and unforeseen events				
total				

Friday........... Saturday........ Sunday...........

weekly expenses

essential expenses

supermarket

other food

pharmacy

transportation

children

pets

total

optional expenses

shopping

cosmetics

gifts

total

entertainment and leisure

books & magazines

music

movies and shows

cafés and takeout

restaurants

total

extras and unforeseen events

medical expenses

travel

total

weekly
total

essential expenses

week 1 ....
week 2 ....
week 3 ....
week 4 ....
week 5 ....
total ....

optional expenses

week 1 ....
week 2 ....
week 3 ....
week 4 ....
week 5 ....
total ....

entertainment and leisure

week 1 ....
week 2 ....
week 3 ....
week 4 ....
week 5 ....
total ....

extras and unforeseen events

week 1 ....
week 2 ....
week 3 ....
week 4 ....
week 5 ....
total ....

utilities

electricity .... phone/Internet ....

gas .... water .... total ....

Pull expenses you entered in the main categories that are substantial (for example, cafés, gas, etc.), if any.

significant expenses

spending on .... spending on ....

week 1 .... week 1 ....
week 2 .... week 2 ....
week 3 .... week 3 ....
week 4 .... week 4 ....
week 5 .... week 5 ....
total .... total ....

summary of monthly expenses

- Compare the totals for all the charts: Which expense categories had the greatest impact this month? Did you expect that?

- Are there expenses you could cut?

----

weekly spending

week 1	------------------
week 2	------------------
week 3	------------------
week 4	------------------
week 5	------------------
utilities	------------------
total monthly spending	------------------

How much cash did you have available? ------------------

How much did you spend? ------------------

How much did you save? ------------------

- Did you reach your goals?   :) Yes   :(No   :| Almost

- If yes, good job! Give yourself a small reward, but don't cancel out all your hard work: choose something that's not too expensive but still makes you happy.

- If no, what went wrong? What could you do next month to improve?

----

month

record your monthly income and spending

income

date	item	amount
total income		

fixed expenses

rent/ mortgage		maintenance/ HOA fees	
bus/subway pass		parking space	
school/ cafeteria		gym	
social insurance contributions		self-employment tax	
total fixed expenses			

goals and forecast

- Which expenses do you plan to cut to save money?

- How can you reach your goals?

How much do you
want to save?

_____

How much money do you have available
this month?

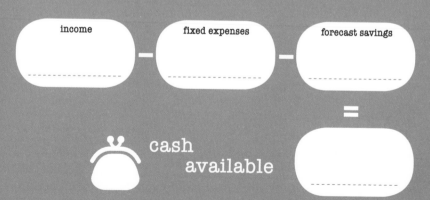

income		fixed expenses		forecast savings

cash available

month

	Monday	Tuesday	Wednesday	Thursday
essential expenses				
optional expenses				
entertainment and leisure				
extras and unforeseen events				
total				

Friday	Saturday	Sunday

weekly expenses

essential expenses

supermarket	
other food	
pharmacy	
transportation	
children	
pets	
total	

optional expenses

shopping	
cosmetics	
gifts	
total	

entertainment and leisure

books & magazines	
music	
movies and shows	
cafés and takeout	
restaurants	
total	

extras and unforeseen events

medical expenses	
travel	
total	

weekly total	

	Monday..........	Tuesday..........	Wednesday.....	Thursday.......
essential expenses				
optional expenses				
entertainment and leisure				
extras and unforeseen events				
total				

Friday	Saturday	Sunday

weekly expenses

essential expenses

supermarket

other food

pharmacy

transportation

children

pets

total

optional expenses

shopping

cosmetics

gifts

total

entertainment and leisure

books & magazines

music

movies and shows

cafés and takeout

restaurants

total

extras and unforeseen events

medical expenses

travel

total

weekly total

	Monday	Tuesday	Wednesday	Thursday
essential expenses				
optional expenses				
entertainment and leisure				
extras and unforeseen events				
total				

Friday..........	Saturday.......	Sunday..........	weekly expenses

weekly expenses

essential expenses

supermarket ....

other food ....

pharmacy ....

transportation ....

children ....

pets ....

....

....

....

total ....

optional expenses

shopping ....

cosmetics ....

gifts ....

....

....

total ....

entertainment and leisure

books & magazines ....

music ....

movies and shows ....

cafés and takeout ....

restaurants ....

....

total ....

extras and unforeseen events

medical expenses ....

travel ....

....

....

total ....

weekly total ....

month _____

	Monday_____	Tuesday_____	Wednesday_____	Thursday_____
essential expenses				
optional expenses				
entertainment and leisure				
extras and unforeseen events				
total				

Friday_____	Saturday_____	Sunday_____

weekly expenses

essential expenses

supermarket	_____
other food	_____
pharmacy	_____
transportation	_____
children	_____
pets	_____
_____	_____
_____	_____
_____	_____
total	_____

optional expenses

shopping	_____
cosmetics	_____
gifts	_____
_____	_____
_____	_____
total	_____

entertainment and leisure

books & magazines	_____
music	_____
movies and shows	_____
cafés and takeout	_____
restaurants	_____
_____	_____
total	_____

extras and unforeseen events

medical expenses	_____
travel	_____
_____	_____
_____	_____
total	_____
weekly total	_____

	Monday	Tuesday	Wednesday	Thursday
essential expenses				
optional expenses				
entertainment and leisure				
extras and unforeseen events				
total				

Friday........... Saturday........ Sunday...........

weekly expenses

essential expenses

supermarket

other food

pharmacy

transportation

children

pets

----

total

optional expenses

shopping

cosmetics

gifts

----

total

entertainment and leisure

books & magazines

music

movies and shows

cafés and takeout

restaurants

----

total

extras and unforeseen events

medical expenses

travel

----

total

weekly total

essential expenses

week 1 ....
week 2 ....
week 3 ....
week 4 ....
week 5 ....
total ....

optional expenses

week 1 ....
week 2 ....
week 3 ....
week 4 ....
week 5 ....
total ....

entertainment and leisure

week 1 ....
week 2 ....
week 3 ....
week 4 ....
week 5 ....
total ....

extras and unforeseen events

week 1 ....
week 2 ....
week 3 ....
week 4 ....
week 5 ....
total ....

utilities

electricity ....   phone/Internet ....

gas ....   water ....   total ....

Pull expenses you entered in the main categories that are substantial (for example, cafés, gas, etc.), if any.

significant expenses

spending on ....   spending on ....

week 1 ....   week 1 ....
week 2 ....   week 2 ....
week 3 ....   week 3 ....
week 4 ....   week 4 ....
week 5 ....   week 5 ....
total ....   total ....

summary of monthly expenses

- Compare the totals for all the charts: Which expense categories had the greatest impact this month? Did you expect that?

- Are there expenses you could cut?

---

weekly spending

week 1	---
week 2	---
week 3	---
week 4	---
week 5	---
utilities	---
total monthly spending	---

How much cash did you have available? ---

How much did you spend? ---

How much did you save? ---

- Did you reach your goals? 😊 Yes 🙁 No 😐 Almost

- If yes, good job! Give yourself a small reward, but don't cancel out all your hard work: choose something that's not too expensive but still makes you happy.

- If no, what went wrong? What could you do next month to improve?

---

month

----

record your monthly income and spending

income

date	item	amount
total income		

fixed expenses

rent/ mortgage		maintenance/ HOA fees	
bus/subway pass		parking space	
school/ cafeteria		gym	
social insurance contributions		self-employment tax	
total fixed expenses			

goals and forecast

- Which expenses do you plan to cut to save money?

_____

_____

- How can you reach your goals?

_____

_____

_____

How much do you
want to save?

_____

How much money do you have available
this month?

income		fixed expenses		forecast savings
	−		−	

cash
available

=

	Monday	Tuesday	Wednesday	Thursday
essential expenses				
optional expenses				
entertainment and leisure				
extras and unforeseen events				
total				

Friday	Saturday	Sunday	weekly expenses

essential expenses

supermarket

other food

pharmacy

transportation

children

pets

total

optional expenses

shopping

cosmetics

gifts

total

entertainment and leisure

books & magazines

music

movies and shows

cafés and takeout

restaurants

total

extras and unforeseen events

medical expenses

travel

total

weekly total

	Monday	Tuesday	Wednesday	Thursday
essential expenses				
optional expenses				
entertainment and leisure				
extras and unforeseen events				
total				

Friday	Saturday	Sunday	weekly expenses

essential expenses

supermarket

other food

pharmacy

transportation

children

pets

total

optional expenses

shopping

cosmetics

gifts

total

entertainment and leisure

books & magazines

music

movies and shows

cafés and takeout

restaurants

total

extras and unforeseen events

medical expenses

travel

total

weekly total

	Monday	Tuesday	Wednesday	Thursday
essential expenses				
optional expenses				
entertainment and leisure				
extras and unforeseen events				
total				

Friday	Saturday	Sunday	weekly expenses

essential expenses

supermarket

other food

pharmacy

transportation

children

pets

total

optional expenses

shopping

cosmetics

gifts

total

entertainment and leisure

books & magazines

music

movies and shows

cafés and takeout

restaurants

total

extras and unforeseen events

medical expenses

travel

total

weekly total

month

	Monday	Tuesday	Wednesday	Thursday
essential expenses				
optional expenses				
entertainment and leisure				
extras and unforeseen events				
total				

Friday_____	Saturday_____	Sunday_____

weekly expenses

essential expenses

supermarket

other food

pharmacy

transportation

children

pets

_____

_____

_____

total

optional expenses

shopping

cosmetics

gifts

_____

_____

total

entertainment and leisure

books & magazines

music

movies and shows

cafés and takeout

restaurants

_____

total

extras and unforeseen events

medical expenses

travel

_____

_____

total

weekly total

month ----------------------------------

	Monday	Tuesday	Wednesday	Thursday
essential expenses				
optional expenses				
entertainment and leisure				
extras and unforeseen events				
total				

Friday........ Saturday........ Sunday........

weekly expenses

essential expenses

supermarket

other food

pharmacy

transportation

children

pets

total

optional expenses

shopping

cosmetics

gifts

total

entertainment and leisure

books & magazines

music

movies and shows

cafés and takeout

restaurants

total

extras and unforeseen events

medical expenses

travel

total

weekly total

essential expenses

week 1 ....
week 2 ....
week 3 ....
week 4 ....
week 5 ....
total ....

optional expenses

week 1 ....
week 2 ....
week 3 ....
week 4 ....
week 5 ....
total ....

entertainment and leisure

week 1 ....
week 2 ....
week 3 ....
week 4 ....
week 5 ....
total ....

extras and unforeseen events

week 1 ....
week 2 ....
week 3 ....
week 4 ....
week 5 ....
total ....

utilities

electricity ....   phone/Internet ....

gas ....   water ....   total ....

Pull expenses you entered in the main categories that are substantial (for example, cafés, gas, etc.), if any.

significant expenses

spending on ....   spending on ....

week 1 ....   week 1 ....
week 2 ....   week 2 ....
week 3 ....   week 3 ....
week 4 ....   week 4 ....
week 5 ....   week 5 ....
total ....   total ....

summary of monthly expenses

- Compare the totals for all the charts: Which expense categories had the greatest impact this month? Did you expect that?

- Are there expenses you could cut?

----

weekly spending

week 1	------------------
week 2	------------------
week 3	------------------
week 4	------------------
week 5	------------------
utilities	------------------
total monthly spending	------------------

How much cash did you have available? ----------------------

How much did you spend? ----------------

How much did you save? ----------------------

- Did you reach your goals?   :) Yes   :(No   :| Almost

- If yes, good job! Give yourself a small reward, but don't cancel out all your hard work: choose something that's not too expensive but still makes you happy.

- If no, what went wrong? What could you do next month to improve?

----

month

_____

record your monthly income and spending

income

date	item	amount

total income	

fixed expenses

rent/ mortgage		maintenance/ HOA fees	
bus/subway pass		parking space	
school/ cafeteria		gym	
social insurance contributions		self-employment tax	

total fixed expenses	

goals and forecast

- Which expenses do you plan to cut to save money?

- How can you reach your goals?

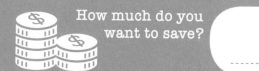

How much do you
want to save?

How much money do you have available
this month?

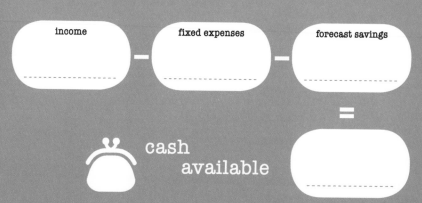

income   fixed expenses   forecast savings

----

cash available

month _____

	Monday	Tuesday	Wednesday	Thursday
essential expenses				
optional expenses				
entertainment and leisure				
extras and unforeseen events				
total				

Friday	Saturday	Sunday

weekly expenses

essential expenses

supermarket	
other food	
pharmacy	
transportation	
children	
pets	
total	

optional expenses

shopping	
cosmetics	
gifts	
total	

entertainment and leisure

books & magazines	
music	
movies and shows	
cafés and takeout	
restaurants	
total	

extras and unforeseen events

medical expenses	
travel	
total	
weekly total	

	Monday	Tuesday	Wednesday	Thursday
essential expenses				
optional expenses				
entertainment and leisure				
extras and unforeseen events				
total				

Friday_____	Saturday_____	Sunday_____

weekly expenses

essential expenses

supermarket	_____
other food	_____
pharmacy	_____
transportation	_____
children	_____
pets	_____
_____	_____
_____	_____
_____	_____
total	_____

optional expenses

shopping	_____
cosmetics	_____
gifts	_____
_____	_____
_____	_____
total	_____

entertainment and leisure

books & magazines	_____
music	_____
movies and shows	_____
cafés and takeout	_____
restaurants	_____
_____	_____
total	_____

extras and unforeseen events

medical expenses	_____
travel	_____
_____	_____
_____	_____
total	_____

weekly total	_____

month ----------------------------------

	Monday_____	Tuesday_____	Wednesday_____	Thursday_____
essential expenses				
optional expenses				
entertainment and leisure				
extras and unforeseen events				
total				

Friday	Saturday	Sunday

weekly expenses

essential expenses

supermarket	
other food	
pharmacy	
transportation	
children	
pets	
total	

optional expenses

shopping	
cosmetics	
gifts	
total	

entertainment and leisure

books & magazines	
music	
movies and shows	
cafés and takeout	
restaurants	
total	

extras and unforeseen events

medical expenses	
travel	
total	

weekly total	

	Monday	Tuesday	Wednesday	Thursday
essential expenses				
optional expenses				
entertainment and leisure				
extras and unforeseen events				
total				

Friday	Saturday	Sunday

weekly expenses

essential expenses

supermarket	
other food	
pharmacy	
transportation	
children	
pets	
total	

optional expenses

shopping	
cosmetics	
gifts	
total	

entertainment and leisure

books & magazines	
music	
movies and shows	
cafés and takeout	
restaurants	
total	

extras and unforeseen events

medical expenses	
travel	
total	

| **weekly total** | |

	Monday	Tuesday	Wednesday	Thursday
essential expenses				
optional expenses				
entertainment and leisure				
extras and unforeseen events				
total				

Friday	Saturday	Sunday	weekly expenses

essential expenses

supermarket _____
other food _____
pharmacy _____
transportation _____
children _____
pets _____
_____ _____
_____ _____
_____ _____

total _____

optional expenses

shopping _____
cosmetics _____
gifts _____
_____ _____
_____ _____

total _____

entertainment and leisure

books & magazines _____
music _____
movies and shows _____
cafés and takeout _____
restaurants _____
_____ _____

total _____

extras and unforeseen events

medical expenses _____
travel _____
_____ _____
_____ _____

total _____

weekly total _____

essential expenses

week 1

week 2

week 3

week 4

week 5

total

optional expenses

week 1

week 2

week 3

week 4

week 5

total

entertainment and leisure

week 1

week 2

week 3

week 4

week 5

total

extras and unforeseen events

week 1

week 2

week 3

week 4

week 5

total

utilities

electricity   phone/Internet

gas   water   total

Pull expenses you entered in the main categories that are substantial (for example, cafés, gas, etc.), if any.

significant expenses

spending on   spending on

week 1   week 1

week 2   week 2

week 3   week 3

week 4   week 4

week 5   week 5

total   total

summary of monthly expenses

- Compare the totals for all the charts: Which expense categories had the greatest impact this month? Did you expect that?

- -

- Are there expenses you could cut?

- -

weekly spending

week 1	- - - - - - - - - - - -
week 2	- - - - - - - - - - - -
week 3	- - - - - - - - - - - -
week 4	- - - - - - - - - - - -
week 5	- - - - - - - - - - - -
utilities	- - - - - - - - - - - -
total monthly spending	- - - - - - - - - - - -

How much cash did you have available? - - - - - - - - - - - - - - - - -

How much did you spend? - - - - - - - - - - - - - - -

How much did you save? - - - - - - - - - - - - - - - - -

- Did you reach your goals?   ☺ Yes   ☹ No   😐 Almost

- If yes, good job! Give yourself a small reward, but don't cancel out all your hard work: choose something that's not too expensive but still makes you happy.

- If no, what went wrong? What could you do next month to improve?

- -

- -

- -

- -

month

_____

record your monthly income and spending

income

date	item	amount
total income		

fixed expenses

rent/ mortgage		maintenance/ HOA fees	
bus/subway pass		parking space	
school/ cafeteria		gym	
social insurance contributions		self-employment tax	
total fixed expenses			

goals and forecast

- Which expenses do you plan to cut to save money?

- How can you reach your goals?

How much do you
want to save?

How much money do you have available
this month?

income	fixed expenses	forecast savings

cash available

month

	Monday	Tuesday	Wednesday	Thursday
essential expenses				
optional expenses				
entertainment and leisure				
extras and unforeseen events				
total				

Friday _____	Saturday _____	Sunday _____	weekly expenses

essential expenses

supermarket	_____
other food	_____
pharmacy	_____
transportation	_____
children	_____
pets	_____
_____	
_____	
_____	
total	_____

optional expenses

shopping	_____
cosmetics	_____
gifts	_____
_____	
_____	
total	_____

entertainment and leisure

books & magazines	_____
music	_____
movies and shows	_____
cafés and takeout	_____
restaurants	_____
_____	
total	_____

extras and unforeseen events

medical expenses	_____
travel	_____
_____	
_____	
total	_____

weekly total	_____

	Monday	Tuesday	Wednesday	Thursday
essential expenses				
optional expenses				
entertainment and leisure				
extras and unforeseen events				
total				

Friday	Saturday	Sunday

weekly expenses

essential expenses

supermarket	
other food	
pharmacy	
transportation	
children	
pets	
total	

optional expenses

shopping	
cosmetics	
gifts	
total	

entertainment and leisure

books & magazines	
music	
movies and shows	
cafés and takeout	
restaurants	
total	

extras and unforeseen events

medical expenses	
travel	
total	
weekly total	

	Monday	Tuesday	Wednesday	Thursday
essential expenses				
optional expenses				
entertainment and leisure				
extras and unforeseen events				
total				

Friday	Saturday	Sunday

weekly expenses

essential expenses

supermarket

other food

pharmacy

transportation

children

pets

total

optional expenses

shopping

cosmetics

gifts

total

entertainment and leisure

books & magazines

music

movies and shows

cafés and takeout

restaurants

total

extras and unforeseen events

medical expenses

travel

total

weekly
total

month _____

	Monday_____	Tuesday_____	Wednesday_____	Thursday_____
essential expenses				
optional expenses				
entertainment and leisure				
extras and unforeseen events				
total				

Friday_____	Saturday_____	Sunday_____	weekly expenses

essential expenses

supermarket	_____
other food	_____
pharmacy	_____
transportation	_____
children	_____
pets	_____
_____	_____
_____	_____
_____	_____
total	_____

optional expenses

shopping	_____
cosmetics	_____
gifts	_____
_____	_____
_____	_____
total	_____

entertainment and leisure

books & magazines	_____
music	_____
movies and shows	_____
cafés and takeout	_____
restaurants	_____
_____	_____
total	_____

extras and unforeseen events

medical expenses	_____
travel	_____
_____	_____
_____	_____
total	_____

weekly total _____

	Monday	Tuesday	Wednesday	Thursday
essential expenses				
optional expenses				
entertainment and leisure				
extras and unforeseen events				
total				

Friday	Saturday	Sunday	weekly expenses

essential expenses

supermarket

other food

pharmacy

transportation

children

pets

total

optional expenses

shopping

cosmetics

gifts

total

entertainment and leisure

books & magazines

music

movies and shows

cafés and takeout

restaurants

total

extras and unforeseen events

medical expenses

travel

total

weekly total

essential expenses

week 1 ....
week 2 ....
week 3 ....
week 4 ....
week 5 ....
total ....

optional expenses

week 1 ....
week 2 ....
week 3 ....
week 4 ....
week 5 ....
total ....

entertainment and leisure

week 1 ....
week 2 ....
week 3 ....
week 4 ....
week 5 ....
total ....

extras and unforeseen events

week 1 ....
week 2 ....
week 3 ....
week 4 ....
week 5 ....
total ....

utilities

electricity ....   phone/Internet ....

gas ....   water ....   total ....

Pull expenses you entered in the main categories that are substantial (for example, cafés, gas, etc.), if any.

significant expenses

spending on ....   spending on ....

week 1 ....   week 1 ....
week 2 ....   week 2 ....
week 3 ....   week 3 ....
week 4 ....   week 4 ....
week 5 ....   week 5 ....
total ....   total ....

summary of monthly expenses

- Compare the totals for all the charts: Which expense categories had the greatest impact this month? Did you expect that?

- Are there expenses you could cut?

weekly spending

week 1	
week 2	
week 3	
week 4	
week 5	
utilities	
total monthly spending	

How much cash did you have available? _____

How much did you spend? _____

How much did you save? _____

- Did you reach your goals? :) Yes :(No :| Almost

- If yes, good job! Give yourself a small reward, but don't cancel out all your hard work: choose something that's not too expensive but still makes you happy.

- If no, what went wrong? What could you do next month to improve?

month

_____

record your monthly income and spending

income

date	item	amount
total income		

fixed expenses

rent/ mortgage		maintenance/ HOA fees	
bus/subway pass		parking space	
school/ cafeteria		gym	
social insurance contributions		self-employment tax	
total fixed expenses			

goals and forecast

- Which expenses do you plan to cut to save money?

- How can you reach your goals?

How much do you
want to save?

How much money do you have available
this month?

income		fixed expenses		forecast savings
	−		−	

cash
available

=

month ....

	Monday.........	Tuesday.........	Wednesday.....	Thursday.......
essential expenses				
optional expenses				
entertainment and leisure				
extras and unforeseen events				
total				

Friday	Saturday	Sunday

weekly expenses

essential expenses

supermarket	
other food	
pharmacy	
transportation	
children	
pets	
total	

optional expenses

shopping	
cosmetics	
gifts	
total	

entertainment and leisure

books & magazines	
music	
movies and shows	
cafés and takeout	
restaurants	
total	

extras and unforeseen events

medical expenses	
travel	
total	

weekly total	

	Monday	Tuesday	Wednesday	Thursday
essential expenses				
optional expenses				
entertainment and leisure				
extras and unforeseen events				
total				

Friday	Saturday	Sunday

weekly expenses

essential expenses

supermarket	
other food	
pharmacy	
transportation	
children	
pets	
total	

optional expenses

shopping	
cosmetics	
gifts	
total	

entertainment and leisure

books & magazines	
music	
movies and shows	
cafés and takeout	
restaurants	
total	

extras and unforeseen events

medical expenses	
travel	
total	

weekly total	

month ....

	Monday..........	Tuesday..........	Wednesday.....	Thursday........
essential expenses				
optional expenses				
entertainment and leisure				
extras and unforeseen events				
total				

Friday	Saturday	Sunday

weekly expenses

essential expenses

supermarket

other food

pharmacy

transportation

children

pets

total

optional expenses

shopping

cosmetics

gifts

total

entertainment and leisure

books & magazines

music

movies and shows

cafés and takeout

restaurants

total

extras and unforeseen events

medical expenses

travel

total

weekly total

	Monday	Tuesday	Wednesday	Thursday
essential expenses				
optional expenses				
entertainment and leisure				
extras and unforeseen events				
total				

Friday	Saturday	Sunday

weekly expenses

essential expenses

supermarket	
other food	
pharmacy	
transportation	
children	
pets	
total	

optional expenses

shopping	
cosmetics	
gifts	
total	

entertainment and leisure

books & magazines	
music	
movies and shows	
cafés and takeout	
restaurants	
total	

extras and unforeseen events

medical expenses	
travel	
total	

weekly total	

month

	Monday	Tuesday	Wednesday	Thursday
essential expenses				
optional expenses				
entertainment and leisure				
extras and unforeseen events				
total				

Friday	Saturday	Sunday

weekly expenses

essential expenses

supermarket	
other food	
pharmacy	
transportation	
children	
pets	
total	

optional expenses

shopping	
cosmetics	
gifts	
total	

entertainment and leisure

books & magazines	
music	
movies and shows	
cafés and takeout	
restaurants	
total	

extras and unforeseen events

medical expenses	
travel	
total	

weekly total	

essential expenses

week 1 ....
week 2 ....
week 3 ....
week 4 ....
week 5 ....
total ....

optional expenses

week 1 ....
week 2 ....
week 3 ....
week 4 ....
week 5 ....
total ....

entertainment and leisure

week 1 ....
week 2 ....
week 3 ....
week 4 ....
week 5 ....
total ....

extras and unforeseen events

week 1 ....
week 2 ....
week 3 ....
week 4 ....
week 5 ....
total ....

utilities

electricity ....   phone/Internet ....

gas ....   water ....   total ....

Pull expenses you entered in the main categories that are substantial (for example, cafés, gas, etc.), if any.

significant expenses

spending on ....

week 1 ....
week 2 ....
week 3 ....
week 4 ....
week 5 ....
total ....

spending on ....

week 1 ....
week 2 ....
week 3 ....
week 4 ....
week 5 ....
total ....

• Compare the totals for all the charts: Which expense categories had the greatest impact this month? Did you expect that?

- -

• Are there expenses you could cut?

- -

weekly spending

week 1	- - - - - - - - - -
week 2	- - - - - - - - - -
week 3	- - - - - - - - - -
week 4	- - - - - - - - - -
week 5	- - - - - - - - - -
utilities	- - - - - - - - - -
total monthly spending	- - - - - - - - - -

How much cash did you have available? - - - - - - - - - - - - - - -

How much did you spend? - - - - - - - - - - - -

How much did you save? - - - - - - - - - - - -

• Did you reach your goals? ☺ Yes ☹ No 😐 Almost

• If yes, good job! Give yourself a small reward, but don't cancel out all your hard work: choose something that's not too expensive but still makes you happy.

• If no, what went wrong? What could you do next month to improve?

- -
- -
- -
- -

annual balance sheet by category

- Fill out this chart with the monthly totals for each of the four main categories, then add them up for your annual totals.

month	essential expenses	optional expenses	entertainment and leisure	extras and unforeseen events
totals	1	2	3	4

- Which month was most difficult? _

- Why? (Possible answers: a lot of unexpected expenses, spent too much on optional items or entertainment, didn't update the kakebo regularly, had problems collecting payments.) _
_ _
_ _

- Which month was easiest? _

- Why? (Possible answers: windfall income, maintained forecast savings, managed to cut some expenses.) _
_ _
_ _

annual balance sheet by category

• Now calculate the percentage for each category. This way you can determine which items have the most impact on your annual budget. Add up the annual totals for all categories and then divide by 100. The answer is *x*.

1 + **2** + **3** + **4**   (divided by 100)   *x*

	÷ 100	=	

• Now divide each total (1, 2, 3, and 4) by *x* for the four expense percentages.

percentage of
essential expenses

| divide **1**
by *x*	=	

percentage of
optional expenses

| divide **2**
by *x*	=	

percentage of
entertainment
and leisure

| divide **3**
by *x*	=	

percentage of
extras and
unforeseen events

| divide **4**
by *x*	=	

• Which expense items had the most impact? _

• Were you aware that you spent more in those categories? _ _ _ _ _ _ _ _ _ _ _ _ _ _ _ _

• Have your spending habits changed since you began using a kakebo? If so, what has changed and why? _
_ _
_ _

• Are there catagories where you could cut spending next year? _ _ _ _ _ _ _ _ _ _ _ _ _
_ _

• Are there catagories where you'd like to or need to invest more? _ _ _ _ _ _ _ _ _ _ _ _
_ _
_ _

annual utilities

- After you've added up your spending in each category at the end of the year, it can be useful to see what the trends are for various utilities. This will help you understand what you spent and why.

Use the monthly summaries (or fixed expenses, if you pay set amounts and recorded your bills at the start of each month) to look at the amounts you paid for electricity, gas, water, and phone service.

electricity

time period	amount
yearly total	
monthly spending	

gas

time period	amount
yearly total	
monthly spending	

water

time period	amount
yearly total	
monthly spending	

phone/Internet

time period	amount
yearly total	
monthly spending	

- Look at the total for each category. Did these figures match your expectations? If not, what surprises you about them? _____

_____

- If you recorded lump-sum amounts, did your spending match your expectation? If not, take a close look at the items and consider whether you should change your plan or consider changing providers.

annual significant expenses

- In the empty boxes below write any substantial expenses. Enter the expenses that you listed at the end of each month in the "significant expenses" box, but also think about cable TV subscriptions, Netflix, Spotify, etc.

  Looking at this breakdown, you may discover, for example, that you spend more than you expected on gas, which might lead you to think about alternatives that could help you save a bit in that area. Or you may discover that the cost of some services is higher than you thought and has more impact than you expected.

spending on _____		spending on _____	
time period	amount	time period	amount
----------------	----------------	----------------	----------------
----------------	----------------	----------------	----------------
----------------	----------------	----------------	----------------
----------------	----------------	----------------	----------------
----------------	----------------	----------------	----------------
----------------	----------------	----------------	----------------
yearly total	----------------	yearly total	----------------
monthly spending	----------------	monthly spending	----------------

spending on _____		spending on _____	
time period	amount	time period	amount
----------------	----------------	----------------	----------------
----------------	----------------	----------------	----------------
----------------	----------------	----------------	----------------
----------------	----------------	----------------	----------------
----------------	----------------	----------------	----------------
----------------	----------------	----------------	----------------
yearly total	----------------	yearly total	----------------
monthly spending	----------------	monthly spending	----------------

- Think about what you've learned so that you can understand how you might improve and make a revised and more effective plan for next year.

annual taxes

- Below, enter your spending during the year on taxes and fees: car registration, waste disposal tax, real estate taxes, and municipal services tax. If you're self-employed, include self-employment tax and your social security and other contributions.

Taxes

item	amount	item	amount
----------------------	------------------	----------------------	------------------
----------------------	------------------	----------------------	------------------
----------------------	------------------	----------------------	------------------
----------------------	------------------	----------------------	------------------
----------------------	------------------	----------------------	------------------
----------------------	------------------	total	------------------

notes

_____

_____

_____

_____

_____

_____

_____

_____

_____

_____

_____

_____

_____

_____

_____

_____

- Draw up an annual balance sheet that summarizes your experiences over the past year. Use it to assess the progress you've made and spot any errors you can correct.

- How much did you save?

MONTHLY SAVINGS

month	amount

total annual savings

Did you achieve your savings goal?

☺ **yes**

😐 **almost**

☹ **no**

- What did you learn from your kakebo? Did you see any improvement in how you manage expenses?

Even if you didn't manage to reach the goal you set, you should celebrate and give yourself a small reward. What will you do with your savings? You could go on a trip, buy something you want, or give a gift to a friend or family member. The possibilities are endless! Let your imagination run wild and enjoy the reward. You've earned it!

If you have more ambitious long-term plans, set aside your savings in a special fund or invest it. When you combine it with next year's savings, you can make an even bigger dream come true!

2019 calendar

JANUARY

SU	M	T	W	TH	F	SA
		1	2	3	4	5
6	7	8	9	10	11	12
13	14	15	16	17	18	19
20	21	22	23	24	25	26
27	28	29	30	31		

FEBRUARY

SU	M	T	W	TH	F	SA
					1	2
3	4	5	6	7	8	9
10	11	12	13	14	15	16
17	18	19	20	21	22	23
24	25	26	27	28		

MARCH

SU	M	T	W	TH	F	SA
					1	2
3	4	5	6	7	8	9
10	11	12	13	14	15	16
17	18	19	20	21	22	23
24	25	26	27	28	29	30
31						

APRIL

SU	M	T	W	TH	F	SA
	1	2	3	4	5	6
7	8	9	10	11	12	13
14	15	16	17	18	19	20
21	22	23	24	25	26	27
28	29	30				

MAY

SU	M	T	W	TH	F	SA
			1	2	3	4
5	6	7	8	9	10	11
12	13	14	15	16	17	18
19	20	21	22	23	24	25
26	27	28	29	30	31	

JUNE

SU	M	T	W	TH	F	SA
						1
2	3	4	5	6	7	8
9	10	11	12	13	14	15
16	17	18	19	20	21	22
23	24	25	26	27	28	29
30						

JULY

SU	M	T	W	TH	F	SA
	1	2	3	4	5	6
7	8	9	10	11	12	13
14	15	16	17	18	19	20
21	22	23	24	25	26	27
28	29	30	31			

AUGUST

SU	M	T	W	TH	F	SA
				1	2	3
4	5	6	7	8	9	10
11	12	13	14	15	16	17
18	19	20	21	22	23	24
25	26	27	28	29	30	31

SEPTEMBER

SU	M	T	W	TH	F	SA
1	2	3	4	5	6	7
8	9	10	11	12	13	14
15	16	17	18	19	20	21
22	23	24	25	26	27	28
29	30					

OCTOBER

SU	M	T	W	TH	F	SA
		1	2	3	4	5
6	7	8	9	10	11	12
13	14	15	16	17	18	19
20	21	22	23	24	25	26
27	28	29	30	31		

NOVEMBER

SU	M	T	W	TH	F	SA
					1	2
3	4	5	6	7	8	9
10	11	12	13	14	15	16
17	18	19	20	21	22	23
24	25	26	27	28	29	30

DECEMBER

SU	M	T	W	TH	F	SA
1	2	3	4	5	6	7
8	9	10	11	12	13	14
15	16	17	18	19	20	21
22	23	24	25	26	27	28
29	30	31				

2020 calendar

JANUARY

SU	M	T	W	TH	F	SA
			1	2	3	4
5	6	7	8	9	10	11
12	13	14	15	16	17	18
19	20	21	22	23	24	25
26	27	28	29	30	31	

FEBRUARY

SU	M	T	W	TH	F	SA
						1
2	3	4	5	6	7	8
9	10	11	12	13	14	15
16	17	18	19	20	21	22
23	24	25	26	27	28	29

MARCH

SU	M	T	W	TH	F	SA
1	2	3	4	5	6	7
8	9	10	11	12	13	14
15	16	17	18	19	20	21
22	23	24	25	26	27	28
29	30	31				

APRIL

SU	M	T	W	TH	F	SA
			1	2	3	4
5	6	7	8	9	10	11
12	13	14	15	16	17	18
19	20	21	22	23	24	25
26	27	28	29	30		

MAY

SU	M	T	W	TH	F	SA
					1	2
3	4	5	6	7	8	9
10	11	12	13	14	15	16
17	18	19	20	21	22	23
24	25	26	27	28	29	30
31						

JUNE

SU	M	T	W	TH	F	SA
	1	2	3	4	5	6
7	8	9	10	11	12	13
14	15	16	17	18	19	20
21	22	23	24	25	26	27
28	29	30				

JULY

SU	M	T	W	TH	F	SA
			1	2	3	4
5	6	7	8	9	10	11
12	13	14	15	16	17	18
19	20	21	22	23	24	25
26	27	28	29	30	31	

AUGUST

SU	M	T	W	TH	F	SA
						1
2	3	4	5	6	7	8
9	10	11	12	13	14	15
16	17	18	19	20	21	22
23	24	25	26	27	28	29
30	31					

SEPTEMBER

SU	M	T	W	TH	F	SA
		1	2	3	4	5
6	7	8	9	10	11	12
13	14	15	16	17	18	19
20	21	22	23	24	25	26
27	28	29	30			

OCTOBER

SU	M	T	W	TH	F	SA
				1	2	3
4	5	6	7	8	9	10
11	12	13	14	15	16	17
18	19	20	21	22	23	24
25	26	27	28	29	30	31

NOVEMBER

SU	M	T	W	TH	F	SA
1	2	3	4	5	6	7
8	9	10	11	12	13	14
15	16	17	18	19	20	21
22	23	24	25	26	27	28
29	30					

DECEMBER

SU	M	T	W	TH	F	SA
		1	2	3	4	5
6	7	8	9	10	11	12
13	14	15	16	17	18	19
20	21	22	23	24	25	26
27	28	29	30	31		

家計簿